Pioneering Space

by Sandra Markle

Illustrated in full color

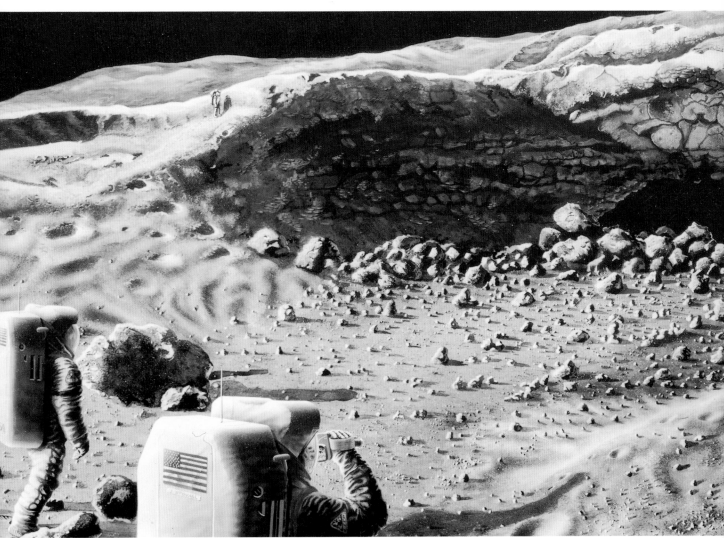

Artist's simulation

ATHENEUM   1992   NEW YORK

Maxwell Macmillan Canada   *Toronto*
Maxwell Macmillan International
New York   Oxford   Singapore   Sydney

For my son Scott as he launches his future—with love!

Acknowledgments:
The author would like to thank the following for sharing their expertise and enthusiasm: Kent Joasten, Lunar and Mars Mission Analyst, National Aeronautics and Space Administration; John W. Dietrich, Ph.D., Lunar Sample Curator, National Aeronautics and Space Administration; and Marc Hairston, Ph.D., Space Physicist, Center for Space Sciences, University of Texas at Dallas.

Photo credits

NASA 1, 2-3, 4, 6, 7, 9, 10, 14, 15, 16, 17, 18, 20, 21, 22, 23, 24, 28, 32, 37b; JPL 25, 26, 27, 35, 36, 37a, 38, 39; Kristina Ahlnäs and Thomas C Royer, U. of Alaska, Fairbanks, supported by NASA 8a; Data by EOSAT, processed by INPE 8b; James Oberg, 12, 13; Steve Foxall Photography 11, 33; EXOS, Inc. 20; Lawrence Livermore National Laboratory 30, 34

Library of Congress Cataloging-in-Publication Data
Markle, Sandra. Pioneering space/Sandra Markle. p. cm. Summary: Describes how space craft work, how space stations function, and how people live in these unusual environments. ISBN 0-689-31748-4 1. Outer space—Exploration —Juvenile literature. [1. Outer space—Exploration.] I. Title. TL793.M313 1992 629.4—dc20 91-24936

Books by
Sandra Markle

Exploring Winter
Exploring Spring
Exploring Summer
Exploring Autumn
Science Mini-Mysteries
Power Up
The Kids' Earth Handbook
Pioneering Space

Artist's simulation

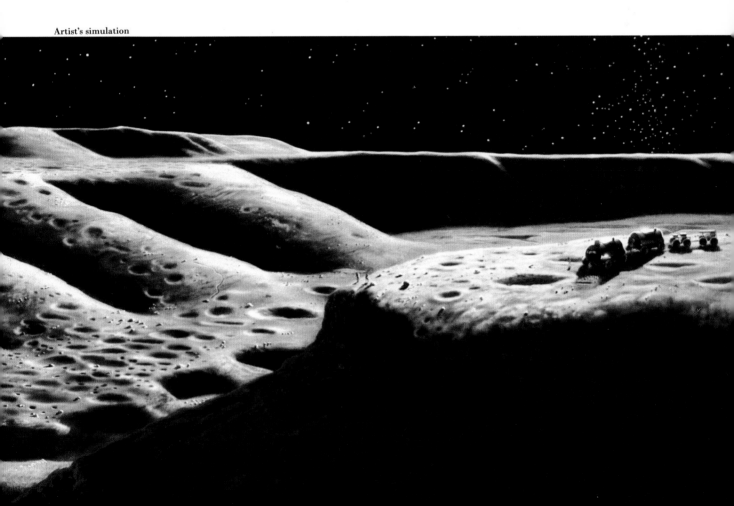

YOU ARE HERE

The arrow in the photograph shows the location of our solar system in the Milky Way Galaxy. Here is the sun, your own home planet Earth with its moon, and all its neighboring planets: Mercury, Venus, Mars, Jupiter, Saturn, Uranus, Neptune, and Pluto. But as you can see there's lots more in space. There are other galaxies, with star-based systems, asteroids, comets, meteors, and many moons. There's even more beyond the range of our ordinary telescopes. It's a whole universe of unexplored wonders.

Earthlings only became spacefarers or voyagers in space some thirty years ago when the Russian Yuri Gagarin spent 108 minutes in orbit on April 12, 1961. Since then more than two hundred men and women from twenty countries have gone into space, but the farthest anyone has ventured from Earth has been about 238,000 miles, the distance the Americans traveled to reach the moon.

Still, it's a beginning.

Adventurous spacefarers will continue to push farther out into the unknown as technological advances provide them the means to do so, but they'll no longer be the only people there. The first pioneers or settlers are moving into space to live and work and even play. The Russians have already had people residing in space for nearly a year at a time aboard their space stations. The United States is working with a multinational group to establish another space station, and there are plans for establishing a lunar base that could be expanded into an environmentally protected town and used for sending an expedition to Mars.

It will still be many years before families board convoys of spacecraft to settle the space frontier, but the era of space pioneering has begun. This book will show you some of the amazing things that have been developed to make moving into space possible and some projects still in the planning stage. As time goes on there will be other projects in which you may one day participate as a space pioneer.

5

The earth is enveloped in a blanket of gases called the atmosphere. The molecules making up these gases are packed tightly together close to the surface and they spread out more and more the farther away from the earth you go. Zooming past sixty thousand feet above the earth's surface, a rocket escapes the clouds and quickly rises to a level where the amount of oxygen in the air is too little for its passengers to breathe and not enough to mix with its fuel supply to keep the engines firing. So a rocket ship must take along its own supply of oxygen. The farther out a craft travels the less dense any remaining atmosphere becomes. Looking at the earth from low earth orbit, the atmosphere will appear as thin bands of colors stacked like a layer cake over the planet's surface and the world immediately surrounding the craft will appear black. Besides having left behind a supply of oxygen, passengers aboard the spacecraft will have lost the protective shield provided by the earth's atmosphere.

Shine a flashlight at a tabletop in a dark room to create a bright spot. Then hold three coffee filters nested together between the flashlight and the table and notice the difference this makes in the light. What you've observed simulates the way the earth's atmosphere filters the radiation that streams out as

The space shuttle Columbia is on its way, leaving the earth behind. Its destination, as much as 250 miles up, is called low earth orbit (LEO).

solar wind from the sun and engulfs the earth. Any craft leaving the protective filter provided by the atmosphere must be shielded against exposure to this radiation. Space pioneers aboard space stations and spacecrafts are partly shielded by the hull, by equipment in their vessel, and by storage tanks of water and fuel. But even these don't provide nearly as effective a block as the earth's atmosphere.

Solar flares cause an even greater threat. These intense bursts of solar radiation can cause people to experience nausea, fatigue, loss of coordination and even to go into a coma. The extent of these reactions, of course, depends on the intensity of the flare and length of time the person is exposed to the radiation. Machines aren't immune either. Exposure to radiation from a solar flare may cause changes in computer microcircuitry called a "soft upset." These changes can trigger unplanned actions in the rockets, such as the firing of thrusters, and the only way to fix it is to reload the programmed memory. Space stations and a lunar colony will need storm cellars or places to protect space pioneers from the especially intense radiation generated by solar flares.

Charged particles streaming out from the sun are trapped by the earth's magnetic force field and flow toward the poles. Sometimes, the charged particles escape and stream down through the atmosphere. When this happens, they appear as glowing sheets of light called auroras. This is a view of an aurora over the southern hemisphere as seen from space. The blue-green and red rays are the aurora lights. The brownish band running along the horizon is called an airglow and is the earth's atmosphere glowing.

Why are computer manufacturers, engineers, doctors, conservationists, city planners, and farmers among those eager for more space pioneering efforts? For one thing, getting away from the earth provides a better view of the planet's surface. This makes it easier to observe land use and plan development, map difficult-to-reach areas, and study the effects of cutting forests and surface mining. Looking down from low earth orbit also makes it possible to spot crop diseases before they've caused widespread damage and to estimate crop yield.

Experiments carried out aboard the Russian Mir space station and the American space shuttle have shown that crystals grown in space are more perfect than those produced on Earth. Scientists hope that studying space-grown crystals of the enzyme isocitrate lyase, for example, may make it possible to develop a new treatment for a plant-attacking fungus.

Other experiments have shown that it's possible to create new types of alloys or combinations of materials in space. Things that normally don't mix on Earth because of their different densities or thicknesses combine freely in microgravity. It's even thought that, one day, mining operations on the moon and on asteroids may provide mineral resources for colonies in space and on Earth.

This satellite image is color enhanced to reveal flow patterns of suspended sediments in the coastal currents in the northern Gulf of Alaska. The clearest water is dark blue and water with the most sediment is peach-colored. Scientists can use this flow information to predict the movement of schools of fish searching for food and to follow the spread of oil spills.

This satellite image reveals the impact farming is having on the Brazilian rain forests. You can see the areas that have been cleared; the image has been processed so they appear tan or brown. Vegetation appears green and water or very wet ground areas appear black.

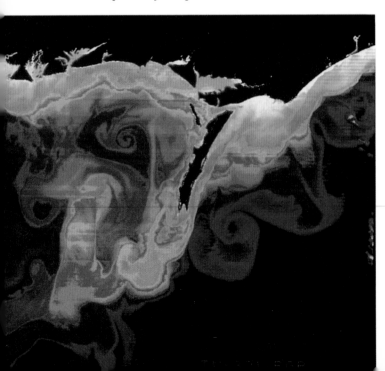

At launch, a rocket's engines must shoot exhaust with a powerful downward thrust. This then propels the rocket ship in the opposite direction—upward. The higher above the surface the rocket must climb the stronger the rocket engine's downward thrust must be to overcome gravity, the force that tugs everything back toward Earth. At lift-off, the shuttle accelerates rapidly within the first fifty seconds to about seven hundred miles per hour. Then as the atmosphere thins, causing less friction against the craft pushing through it, the shuttle continues to gain speed until it's traveling over seventeen thousand miles per hour by the time it reaches its orbital level. No wonder it takes an external tank as big as a farm silo plus a pair of solid rocket boosters to fuel this launch.

The space shuttle or any object is able to remain in orbit when the distance it falls back toward the earth in a given amount of time is equal to the distance the earth's curved surface has turned away under it during that time. So the shuttle or object literally keeps on falling all the way around the earth. That's why to return to Earth, the shuttle fires its rockets to brake it slightly, allowing gravity to pull it home. That's also why, to escape Earth's gravity and go to the moon, the American astronauts had to use an even bigger, more powerful rocket called the Saturn V. And while the Saturn V has not been used since the last Skylab mission in 1974, the Russians have

Just like any combustion engine on Earth, the shuttle's engines can't fire without oxygen. This space-bound craft must take along its own supply to mix with the fuel for two reasons. First, the engines burn fuel so quickly at the time of lift-off that it would be impossible to draw in enough oxygen from the air. And then the shuttle quickly rises to a level of the atmosphere where very little oxygen is available.

developed a new powerful rocket called the Energiya. But instead of sending ships farther into space, Energiya's purpose is to lift the heavy parts of the space station Mir into orbit. Eventually, Mir may be the starting point for a mission to Mars. Launching from orbit would require much less fuel because at this distance from Earth the spacecraft is already up to about 75 percent of the speed needed to reach escape velocity—about twenty-five hundred miles per hour.

Artist's simulation

The X-30 is one of the designs currently being considered for a new generation of aerospace planes. These planes will be able to fly in the upper atmosphere at superfast speeds—faster by far than any aircraft has yet flown. They also would be able to take off from a runway and rise to low earth orbit, returning later to land on a conventional airport runway. To accomplish such feats, new supersonic jet engines will need to be designed. And the plane will need to be constructed with special high-strength, low-weight, heat-resistant materials.

You can see for yourself how a rocket launches by building a balloon rocket. Collect a plastic straw, a nine-inch balloon, masking tape, scissors, monofilament fishing line, and a chair. Ask a friend to help you.

Tie one end of a piece of fishing line at least eight feet long to a point as high as you can reach safely. Next, cut the straw in half crosswise, thread the free end of the line through the straw, and tie the line to a chair. Move the chair to stretch the line tight. Blow up the balloon until it's about halfway expanded. Pinch the neck shut and place the side of the inflated balloon against the straw on the fishing line. Hold the balloon in place while your partner anchors it with a strip of tape. Then let go of the balloon's neck.

Feel the air escape out the neck as the balloon shoots away in the opposite direction and notice how far up the line the rocket climbs before it starts to fall back. What do you think you could do to make the balloon rocket climb even higher?

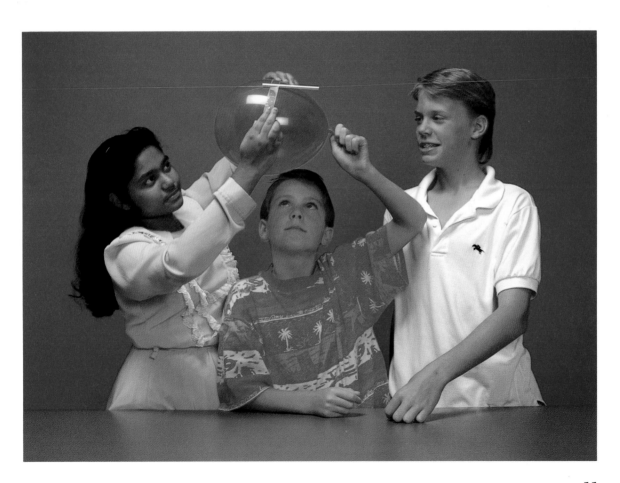

11

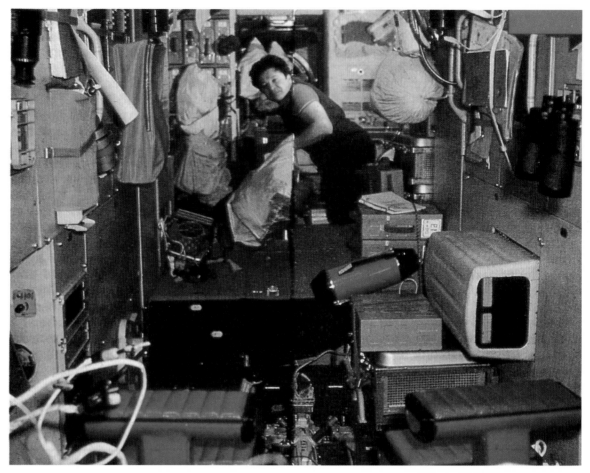

Leonid Kizim, who was the first Mir commander, is in the aft section of the space station. You can see food cabinets on the right and at the very back is the hatch where supply ships link up. Kizim is busy stowing spare equipment.

The Soviets have the first modular space habitat, because segments have gradually been added to Mir, the core station. At first, Mir was both the experimental work area and living quarters for the crew. Solar panels supply power and an antenna allows a communications link. Later, three modules were added. Quant is an observatory, Quant 2 is a service module with additional experimental equipment, and Crystal contains completely automated machines to grow crystals and instruments to measure solar radiation. There are plans to add two more modules that will be used to conduct observations of the earth and study the planet's environmental problems. Supply vehicles dock at one end of Mir, and the Soyuz craft ferrying crews to and from the space station dock at the other end.

12

The Mir space station is rather like a research outpost. Crews come and go aboard the Soyuz spacecraft. Food, including fresh fruits and vegetables, water, and propellants, plus any necessary special equipment for mission experiments, are delivered to the station by special cargo vehicles named Progress. As these supplies are used up, they're replaced by trash, and when the transfer is complete, the Progress freighter is de-orbited. A short time later, a new Progress vessel docks with another load of supplies.

While on board Mir, cosmonauts carry out a variety of experiments and operations. For example, they grow crystals and investigate how aerosols behave in weightlessness. They also study the effect of long-term exposure to weightlessness on human subjects—themselves. They take photos of Earth and study its surface features. Several different types of special telescopes were mounted on Mir as part of a multinational cooperative space study.

Yuri Romenenko is doing exercises to study how the lung and heart function while in space. With an eleven month stay, Romenenko was the first person to remain in space longer than six or seven months. The current record is a year, but Mir crews generally only spend about six months at a time in space.

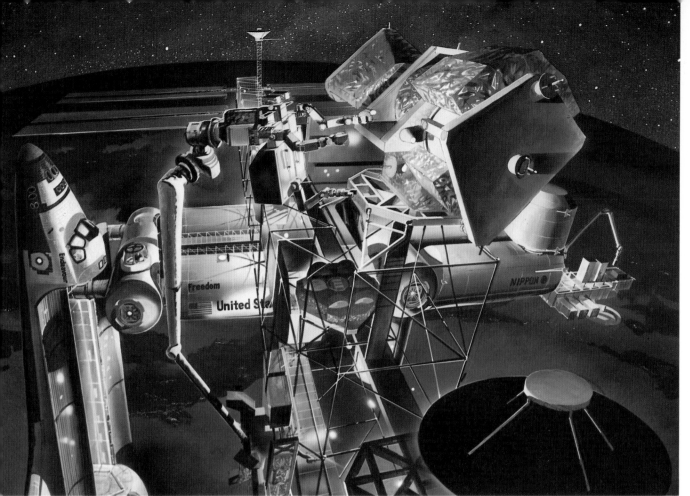

Artist's simulation

The space station Freedom being produced through the combined effort of the United States, Canada, Japan, Italy, and the European Space Agency may not look exactly like this once it's built, but it will be very close to this design. In the artist's drawing you can see the shuttle docked at the station. Look closely and you'll spot an astronaut inside the cupola near the space shuttle. He is controlling the flight telerobotic servicer. This remote-controlled device makes it possible to perform tasks outside the station while the operator remains safely inside.

The section that bears the words UNITED STATES is the habitat module complete with many of the comforts of home. There is a cabin for each of the four crew members. These cabins are on the ceiling, along the walls, and on the floor because in microgravity there is no sense of being upside down. There are also laundry facilities, a microwave/convection oven, a refrigerator/freezer, and a trash compactor. The section labeled Nippon is one of several modules for experimental work that are held together by a supporting truss. As in Mir, panels of solar cells supply the station's power.

14

You've already discovered that space stations depend on solar energy for power. The sun will also be the most likely power source for future colonies on the moon, Mars, or even asteroids. There's plenty of solar energy available in space, and solar cells make it possible to easily trap radiation and convert it to electricity.

The solar cells are made of extremely thin wafers sliced from a silicon crystal that has been treated with two special chemicals. This treatment creates a wafer that has two distinctly different regions—one with atoms that have more electrons than usual and one with atoms that have fewer electrons than usual. Normally, atoms, the tiny building blocks of matter, are balanced: made up of an equal number of negatively charged particles called electrons and positively charged particles called protons. Because of this imbalance in the wafer, light energy striking it causes a reaction. The extra electrons gain enough energy to flow into the other layer, which has a shortage of electrons, and there they are absorbed. This flow of electrons is an electric current. The amount of electricity produced depends on the intensity of the light energy striking the cell and on the size of the solar cell.

Space station Freedom will use solar arrays or panels of solar cells to provide the supply of electrical power it needs. Special nickel hydrogen batteries will store power for use during periods when the cells aren't exposed to solar radiation.

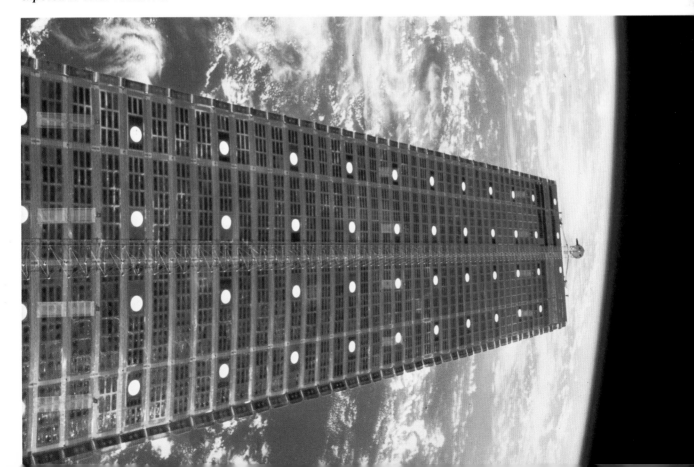

Since space doesn't provide the things we use on Earth, anyone going into space must take along everything needed to survive. Or they must be able to produce what's needed.

For one thing, a space habitat must have an atmosphere with a mixture of gases including oxygen and nitrogen. Although we need to breath oxygen to survive, breathing pure oxygen can damage our lungs. The atmosphere in the habitat must be dense enough to exert the right amount of pressure so that the air that's breathed is forced into the air sacs of the lungs. It's from these sacs that the oxygen is picked up by the blood and carried to the body's cells.

Since spacecrafts are sealed, maintaining a livable atmosphere means

To shower in space, the bather will need to spread on a pastelike soap. Next, water will be squirted on, pushed around, and then suctioned up. The bather finishes by suctioning up any drops remaining inside the shower and then dries off with a blast of warm air.

that the waste carbon dioxide gas that people breathe out needs to be removed. This is done by circulating the air through canisters containing lithium hydroxide. This chemical acts like a "molecular sponge" to absorb the waste gases. Additional oxygen is released as needed, and the amount of humidity in the air is also regulated.

Besides providing shelter from the extreme temperatures outside, the spacecraft must be able to rid itself of the excess heat given off by the people and machines trapped inside the tightly sealed vessel. Radiators mounted on the inside of the cargo bay doors transfer the extra heat into space. That's why the space shuttles orbit with the cargo bay doors open. The Soviet Soyuz spacecraft has a wall-mounted radiator to control air temperature.

Without gravity to carry wastes away, a strong air current is automatically activated when the commode is in use to propel wastes into a containment compartment. Solid wastes are compacted and stored for return to Earth. Liquid wastes are treated and recycled in a system kept separate from the drinking water. The bubble above the toilet is a special hand-washing device.

The astronaut is chasing down his orange juice. Without Earth's gravitational pull, the only force tugging on the juice molecules is their own attraction for each other. The molecules pull together into the shape that contains the most volume for the least possible surface area—a sphere.

If you've ever ridden a roller coaster, you've experienced weightlessness. It was the feeling you had as you plunged down a steep incline. Although the roller coaster car was on the track, it was as if you'd been tossed up to a great height and then allowed to fall back to the earth's surface. As you'll remember, that's what happens in space too. You're falling without landing. Because while you're falling you aren't noticeably affected by the force of gravity, you float weightless. Actually, gravity still has a tiny influence, so more precisely you're experiencing microgravity.

Besides being light enough to float, your body goes through some physical changes in microgravity. The cartilage discs separating the bones in your spinal column aren't pressed together the way they are on Earth, so in space, people are as much as 1.5 inches taller. Waistlines are also thinner, but faces are much puffier. Those changes happen because the body's fluids shift toward the head. Some people also suffer from a condition called space adaptation syndrome, which makes them feel depressed, very tired, and nauseated. Scientists believe this problem may be caused by the fact that in space there is no definite feeling of being up or down. Fortunately, most people recover within a couple of days.

Because space is a totally hostile environment for people, scientists have developed tools that make it possible to work in space without actually being there. One such tool is a fifty-foot-long remote manipulator arm that operates out of the shuttle's cargo bay. Safely inside, looking out a window, the person operating the arm uses controls much the way you might interact with a computer game. The operator's hand movements cause electric motors to manipulate the arm's shoulder, elbow, and wrist joints. There are also special controls to manipulate the arm's mechanical version of a hand.

The malfunctioning System IV-3 communication satellite was captured, brought into the shuttle's cargo bay for repairs, and released. To make sure it was clear of the shuttle, this astronaut got a lift up by the remote manipulator arm and gave the satellite a shove.

Each sensor of the Dexterous Hand Master picks up three different bending motions plus side-to-side movements of each part of the hand. Work is underway to develop a tool that also allows the user to control a robot's elbow and shoulder movements.

With the help of the latest computer technology, a new tool makes it even easier to remotely control a robot hand. The Dexterous Hand Master has a metal exoskeleton that attaches by loops to each finger joint, the thumb, and the wrist. Each metal section of the exoskeleton glove has tiny sensors that "detect" changes in the angles of the parts of the hand. A computer translates this position data into control commands that are transmitted to a robot. This handy tool is capable of more than the gross movements accomplished by the remote manipulator arm. It can control a robot's hand precisely enough to catch a ball and operate a tool. Scientists are working on a system that would let the person wearing the glove sense resistance to movement when the robot hand touches something. This "touch" sense would make it possible for the worker to have enough control over the robot to perform tasks as delicate as picking up an egg without crushing it.

On the surface of another planet or moon, the robot could be used to collect rock samples or operate mining equipment while the astronaut controller stays in a safe environment.

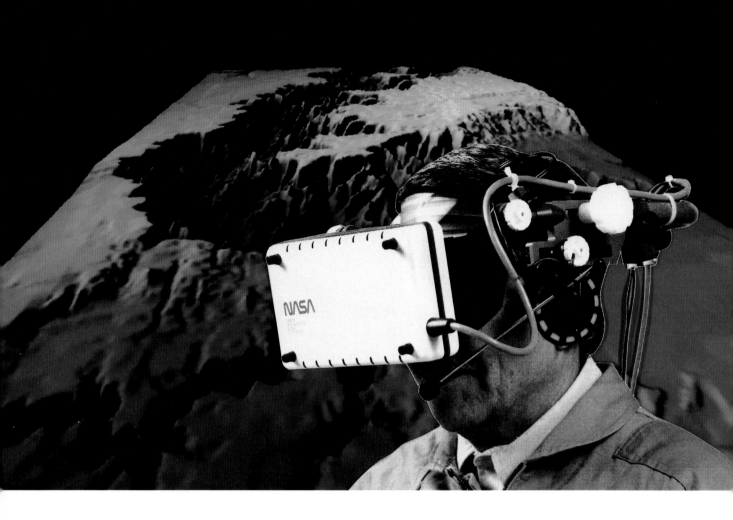

Scientists at NASA's Ames Research Center have found a way to make remotely controlling a robot's movements even more like actually performing the task. A head-mounted screen and ear phones let the wearer see a three-dimensional computer-generated image of what the robot "sees" with twin cameras, and hear any sounds the robot's sensors pick up. In response to head movements, the cameras move, letting the person look up, down, left, or right. Called telepresence or a virtual environment workstation, this artificial reality lets a space worker get the feel of actually being on the job. Dressed in a special "data suit," the worker then goes through the motions of performing whatever task is to be accomplished. A computer translates these movements into commands that are transmitted to the robot to make it mimic the worker's actions. Or the worker can simply issue voice commands telling the robot what to do.

20

Because space station operations are likely to require extensive extravehicular activity, there has been a concern about how to retrieve irreplaceable equipment or even more importantly an astronaut who becomes untethered. The space station wouldn't be able to engage in a chase, a shuttle craft might not be available, and readying an astronaut in a manned maneuvering unit could take too long. Such a manned rescue effort could also endanger the person attempting the retrieval. It was decided that what was needed was a robot that could respond to simple voice commands, such as "quick activate," "search," and "grapple." Then based on the command, the robot should be able to act on its own to successfully carry out its rescue mission.

This picture of the EVA Retriever is an artist's simulation. The real thing is still being developed. One of the most difficult developmental jobs is to provide the robot with visual perception so it can both avoid obstacles and grasp the variety of different targets it might have to retrieve. Vision is such a powerful sense for people and as easy to use as just looking around. For a robot to have even a limited visual sense, though, requires computer hardware and software capable of storing an enormous volume of data and processing it extremely fast. Another key element being developed for the EVA Retriever is a "smart" hand. This version of the dexterous hand would be automatically activated when sensors determined the object being retrieved was within range. The hand would then successfully grab the object—it's hoped, on the first attempt.

Artist's simulation

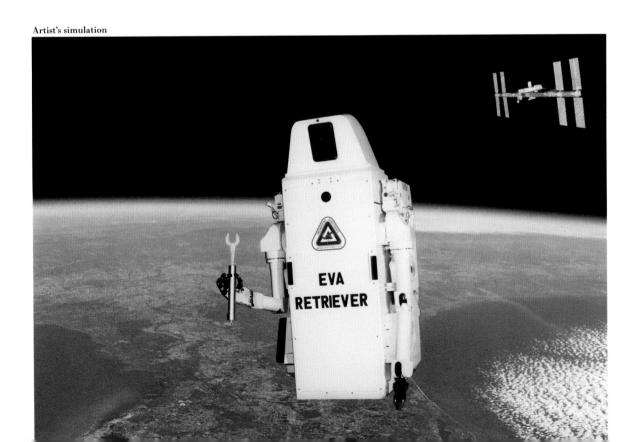

When a human space worker actually does have to go out into space or onto the surface of the moon or another planet, he or she will need a space suit. The suit will need to provide an earthlike environment plus a shield against solar radiation and micrometeoroids.

Actually, a space suit isn't just one thing; it's a series of garments. Innermost is a waste containment system because once someone is dressed in a space suit and out in space, it isn't easy to come inside and go to the bathroom. Over this and next to the skin is a suit that's like stretchy pajamas with thin plastic tubes laced into the fabric. Cool water circulating through these tubes helps keep the space suit wearer from overheating. Then there are soft nylon gloves and a skull cap to keep the rigid suit from rubbing against sensitive skin.

Even the pressure suit is made up of layers. An inner layer of nylon and urethane-coated nylon acts like a balloon to hold the air inside the suit. Without this layer in the near vacuum of space, the greater air pressure inside the suit would push outward to make the suit swell until it burst. This air-filled layer makes it awkward and tiring to move, though. Try bending a long blown-up balloon and you'll see how it feels to bend gloved fingers in a spacesuit.

The outermost layers are mylar separated by layers of dacron to provide protection from temperature

This is one of the latest U.S. space suit designs called the ZPS Mark-3. Like Russian suits, this model can be put on simply by opening a door in the back and climbing inside. The ZPS Mark-3 also has an inside air pressure that's closer to Earth's, so there's less risk than in the low-pressure suits of carbon dioxide bubbling out of the blood and painfully collecting in joints. And the ZPS Mark-3 has new special cloth-and-ball-bearing joints to make it easier to move despite the greater interior pressure.

extremes and from exposure to solar radiation. These layers are topped with Teflon to keep micrometeoroids from puncturing the suit and to prevent bumps and scrapes from tearing it. And the torso of the suit is rigid fiberglass to support the backpack-style life support system.

Finally, there is a helmet with a visor to protect against infrared and ultraviolet light since there's no atmosphere to filter out these harmful rays. Inside, there is a communication cap containing earphones and a microphone. There's also a drinking water bag with a straw and a port through which food can be sucked.

Think it would be fun to go off on your own in space? The manned maneuvering unit (MMU) makes it possible to do that safely.

Shaped like an oversized rigid backpack, the MMU has two "arms" with hand controllers that can be activated by being tapped, pulled, or pushed—the kinds of movements easiest to manage when dressed in a space suit. When a controller is activated, nitrogen gas is released, like someone squirting a spray can. That's all the force necessary to propel the MMU and its rider in space at a speed that is about the same as riding a department store escalator.

James van Hoften, an astronaut who used the MMU to go out from the shuttle and repair a satellite, described what it was like to be alone in space. "Nothing prepares you for the unique sensation of seeing the earth going around under you or looking out into the void of space. Space is so black it's hard to describe how black it is—even in the middle of the day. And the earth looks huge below you. You can see storm patterns, ocean wave patterns, and dark splotches which are cities."

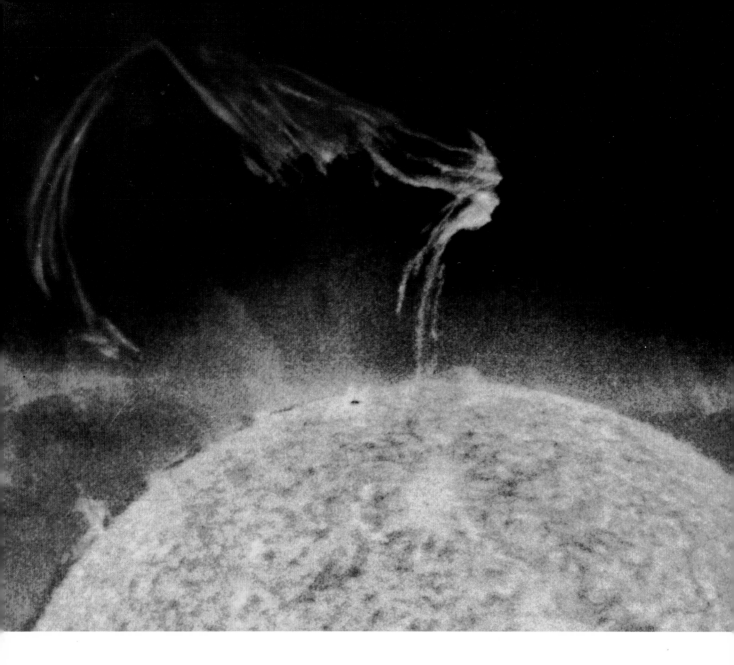

The solar system has special features that may one day be attractions for space tourists. Among the most spectacular of these, of course, are solar flares or huge eruptions of solar gases. Such flares may extend out from the sun's surface as much as sixty-two thousand miles and release as much energy as ten million hydrogen bombs. It's no wonder that when these bursts of charged particles reach Earth they disrupt telephone communication and radio signals. People in space or on planets or moons that don't have the protection of an atmosphere would need to be inside specially shielded shelters during solar flare activity.

Flying by Mars, the fourth planet out from the sun, it would be possible to view two of the solar system's wonders at one time: the largest volcano and the biggest canyon.

Olympus Mons, the largest volcano ever discovered, is a shield volcano like Mauna Loa, the largest volcano on Earth. Shield volcanoes form as relatively gentle eruptions pour lava out on the planet's surface rather than spewing it explosively into the air. Mauna Loa, however, is only seventy-two miles across at its base, rises about six miles from the bottom of the ocean, and has a summit crater that is about a mile and a half wide. Olympus Mons is over three hundred miles across at its base, rises nearly thirteen miles, and has a summit crater nearly fifty miles wide.

Valles Marineris dwarfs any other canyon discovered in the solar system so far, including Earth's Grand Canyon. Valles Marineris is about three thousand miles long, varies from eighty to four hundred miles across, and at some places is more than five miles deep. The Grand Canyon, on the other hand, is only about two hundred miles long, from four to eighteen miles wide, and about a mile deep. Valles Marineris is located near the planet's equator and along the western end of the huge uplifted area that includes Olympus Mons and other smaller volcanoes. Scientists believe that the forces that pushed up this region caused the fracturing that created the canyon. Over time, slumping and landslides enlarged it to its current amazing proportions.

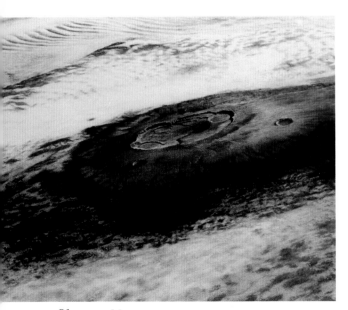

Olympus Mons

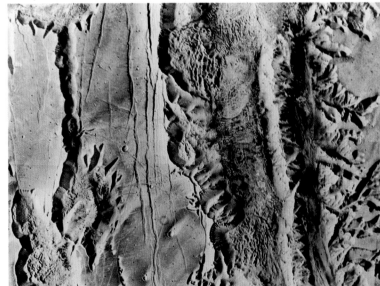

Section of Valles Marineris

Space gazers have always been fasci-
nated by the planet Saturn's rings.
Satellite probes Voyager I and II
revealed what a beautiful sight these
are for travelers who can get a close
look. These halolike rings, which
stretch out from close to the planet's
surface nearly 84,700 miles, are actually
extremely thin and made up of thou-
sands of ringlets. Each ringlet is
composed of separately orbiting frag-
ments of light-reflecting material
thought to be water ice. These frag-
ments range in size from specks to
house-sized chunks. In some sections of
the rings, the ice seems to contain a
dark tint, which may be dirt, or a
reddish coloring, which may be traces
of rust.

26

Mercury, the planet closest to the sun, has a crust that appears to be peppered with craters. Scientists believe these were formed when meteoroids or other chunks of solid matter traveling through space slammed into Mercury's surface. This has happened to other moons and planets, including the earth, but the surface of Mercury, which is only about the size of the moon, is literally covered with them.

You can see for yourself how craters form. Find five pebbles ranging in size from about the size of the end of your little finger to as big as a quarter. Fill a shoe box about half full of sand. Mix in just enough water to make the sand pack together and smooth out the surface. Working outdoors or in an area covered with newspapers, hold the pebbles one by one about six to eight inches above the box and drop them into the sand. Watch closely as the pebbles strike. Do you see some sand splash as it's pushed out? What happened to the sand where the pebble hit? Now, try dropping pebbles from greater heights or add force as you let go.

Even though Mercury's surface is hard rather than soft like the wet sand, the effect is much the same. The impact creates a crater. Some meteoroids, like some of the pebbles, strike with greater force, digging deeper holes. Sometimes the impact also sends debris splattering. Most of the original meteoroid material breaks up on impact.

One area on Mercury, which covers more than twenty-three thousand square miles, is so broken that the crust appears to have been torn and tossed into choppy piles.

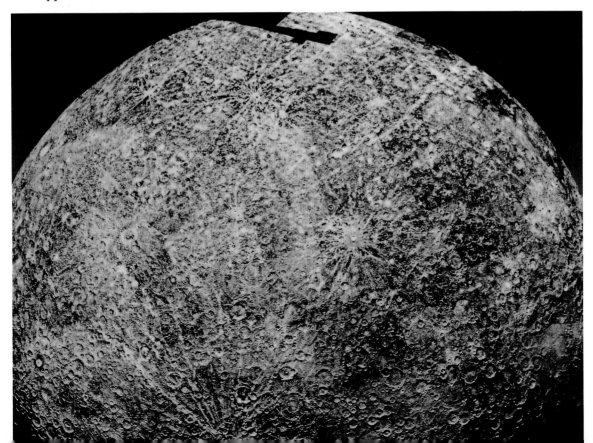

Weather enthusiasts won't want to miss flying by Jupiter, the largest planet in the solar system. The giant red spot that can be viewed there is really the solar system's most gigantic storm. Although it has been observed to vary slightly, it's usually about the size of two Earth-sized circles placed next to each other. No one knows for sure how long this storm has been raging, but the giant red spot has been observed on Jupiter for centuries.

You may be surprised to learn that until 1959, when a Soviet satellite took the first photos, no one had ever seen what is called the far side of the moon. Like the earth, the moon revolves as it orbits. The moon, though, turns very slowly so it takes about the same length of time to complete one revolution as it does to finish one trip around the earth. Because the timing is so nearly the same, the moon always appears to keep the same side toward the earth. To see how this happens, mark an ink spot on one side of a tennis ball. Then let one of your hands balled into a fist represent the earth. Hold the ball so the ink spot is facing your earth-hand and rotate it very slowly while you propel the ball in a circle around your hand. If you make the ball revolve slowly enough, the ink spot will always be facing your earth-hand.

Both sides of the moon are made up of the same basic features, though: craters and maria. The craters, as you discovered, were formed by meteoroids striking the surface. Some are so tiny they're less than an inch across; others, called basins, are more than a hundred miles across. The maria are large, flatter regions. Scientists believe that the maria were the result of lava flows filling immense crater basins at some time in the moon's ancient past. There are mountain ranges around maria, which are believed to have been formed by rock thrown out by the impact of a meteoroid and dome-shaped mountains that scientists believe are inactive volcanoes. There are also rilles or long valleys and narrow ridges. The entire lunar surface is covered with a layer made mostly of broken bits of moon rock called regolith. There are few meteoroids; most of them vaporized upon impact.

On the left is the side of the moon you can see from Earth. This is also the only side people have explored. American astronauts landed at six different sites, studied the immediate vicinity, and brought back a total of about 840 pounds of rock for scientists to analyze and study. The view on the right of the far side of the moon reveals that it has more craters than the front.

Artist's simulation

This plan for a lunar base being developed by researchers at Lawrence Livermore National Laboratory uses inflatable dwellings made out of a superstrong material called Kevlar. After being removed from the transport vehicle and set up, the base would be buried by a teleoperated lunar soilmover. This would provide a protective shield against meteorites and harmful solar radiation. Next, the crew would set up a solar cell array to provide the base's electrical power. Then they would install interior walls, floors, plumbing, and wiring, turning the modules into their lunar homes.

There are several other ideas about how a lunar base should be built. The main goal of each design, though, is to provide protection against the moon's harsh environment, particularly temperature extremes and solar radiation.

One plan calls for building the lunar base out of modular units that would be transported in ready-to-move-in condition from the earth to the moon. The lunar rovers and trailers, which would be sent up in advance to help scientists select a base site, would first be used to dig trenches. The modular units would be placed in these trenches when they arrived and the units would be linked together by air locks. Then regolith would be piled over the base to shield it. Scientists estimate that a layer three to six feet thick would be needed to provide adequate protection against normal solar radiation. Solar storm shelters would need to be built to provide a safe haven during solar flare activity.

Another base design would eliminate the need to bury the colony or build storm shelters. According to this plan, an inflatable habitat would be set up inside one of the moon's lava tubes. Lava tubes also exist in volcanic regions on Earth. They form when a stream of molten lava begins to cool so quickly that it hardens on the outside while the hot material inside continues to flow. After the lava flow stops, a hollow tube is left. While all Earth's lava tubes are relatively small, cavernous ones may exist on the moon as remnants of a volcanically active ancient past. Since the tube's walls would be many feet thick, a base set up inside the tube would be adequately shielded from even the most intense solar radiation. Temperatures would also be likely to remain constant at about –5° F.

Besides deciding how to build a colony, scientists are also trying to decide where to build a lunar base. The Sea of Tranquility near where Apollo 11 landed is being considered. Another choice is near one of the poles. A polar location near a crater would be a good site for a solar power station. Except for eclipses, when the earth passes between the moon and the sun blocking the light, the sun would always be above the horizon and shining on the solar array.

This Controlled Ecological Life Support System (CELSS) at the Kennedy Space Center is one of several experiments being conducted by scientists working to develop a way for space pioneers to grow fresh vegetables. Dwarf varieties of plants with similar requirements for temperature, amount of humidity, nutrients, and exposure to sunlight are grown in the "space garden." Nutrients and water are delivered to the plant roots by a soilless water-based system called hydroponics. Artificial light replaces sunlight and humidity is regulated by recycling water given off by the plants' leaves. Since green growing plants give off oxygen, a space garden could also help furnish oxygen for space travelers and colonists. One of the challenges of making the space garden work is finding a way to keep the fluid in the system around the roots instead of floating off in the microgravity of space.

You can see for yourself what it's like to raise plants hydroponically. You'll need a plastic foam cup, a plastic butter tub with a snap-on plastic lid, sharp scissors, enough vermiculite to fill the cup, liquid fertilizer, a one-inch-by-ten-inch strip of a clean old cotton T-shirt, three bean seeds (you can substitute dried soup beans but be sure to use ones that are whole), and a soup bowl.

Carefully cut a slot in the bottom of the cup and in the lid of the tub just big enough for the cotton strip to slide through. Fill the tub two-thirds full of water and add liquid fertilizer according to the package directions. Thread the cotton strip a little more than halfway up the inside of the cup and hold it in place while you pour in the vermiculite. Place the other end of this wick strip through the slot in the lid into the tub of water and snap on the lid, easing the cup into position on top of it.

Next, place the bean seeds in the bowl, cover with tap water, and soak overnight. Then plant the seeds by poking three holes in the vermiculite, putting a seed in each, and covering them with vermiculite. Place the hydroponic system in a warm, sunny location. You should see sprouts within a few days. Add more water and fertilizer to the container as needed and watch your plants grow.

According to one plan for how the moon's supply of helium-3 could be mined, a machine would first scoop up the regolith. Inside the machine, heat collected from the sun by a nearby solar disk and beamed to the mining machine would make the lunar soil hot enough to drive off the gases. These would be collected by a compressor and stored in cylinders. The processed regolith would then be returned to the moon's surface.

Setting up a lunar base may provide more than an opportunity to explore Earth's closest neighbor firsthand. Scientists now believe that the moon may be the source of a new fuel.

Since the moon doesn't have an atmosphere or a magnetic field to shield it, its surface has been constantly bombarded by solar radiation. Space probes have shown that this solar wind contains particles of a type of helium called helium-3. Based on this and the fact that the lunar rocks brought back by the lunar missions contained a lot of these helium-3 particles, scientists estimate that lunar regolith could be a rich source of this material. Helium-3 can be used in nuclear fusion, a way to release energy from particles by joining them. The helium can be joined with another material called deuterium to produce energy to make electricity. This reaction happens without producing any harmful radioactive wastes. Besides helium-3, mining lunar regolith would also yield oxygen, nitrogen, hydrogen, and carbon dioxide. The helium-3 would be transported back to Earth, but the other gases could be used by lunar colonists for life-support systems and to help cultivate plants in the base's greenhouse.

Here's the planet Mars as viewed by the Viking satellite. This planet has long held a great fascination for Earth's residents and is now considered the next target for new space exploration. Although scientists may eventually find some useful resource, the mission's primary goal is to investigate Mars firsthand.

The main problem holding up a Mars mission is the length of time needed for a round trip. To intercept Mars in its orbital path around the sun, land, and then loop back to connect with Earth once again will take two to three years, using current rockets. And that travel time is still based on assembling and launching a rocket from a space station so that it isn't necessary to use a lot of fuel to escape Earth's gravity.

No one is sure what effect spending such long periods of time exposed to microgravity conditions would have on the human body. There's also the problem of transporting all the food, water, and oxygen a crew would need for such a long mission, and the fact that such a mission would require the crew to be away from home for a very long time.

Before any manned mission to Mars can be considered, though, scientists want to send more unmanned probes to collect information about the planet and its atmosphere. They want to be sure that any Mars dust that might be carried on a space suit into a habitat won't be toxic or contain disease-causing bacteria. They also want to understand conditions on Mars well enough to be able to consider what effect there might be from any bacteria human explorers carry onto the surface.

One of the things scientists already know about Mars is that the soil really is as red as it appears in this sunset view. The soil is this color because it contains a lot of iron and oxygen, and when iron is exposed to oxygen it produces an orangish red rust.

Since it's farther from the sun than Earth, Mars is a much colder planet, with temperatures averaging far below the lowest temperature ever recorded on Earth. Each year as Mars reaches its closest point to the sun, though, daytime temperatures climb. Then the difference between daytime and night-time temperatures becomes extreme. This generates hurricane force winds that blow blizzards of red dust. Sometimes these dust storms continue for more than an earth month. Such storms could cause serious problems for members of a Mars mission trying to explore the planet.

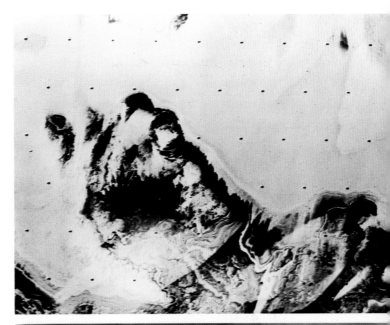

These ice cliffs are at Mars's North Pole. Observations have revealed that most of this ice isn't frozen water, though. It's frozen carbon dioxide, like dry ice. In fact, it "snows" dry ice at the poles during the wintertime.

The tiny amounts of water vapor in the air on Mars are enough to create fogs that cling in canyons and form thin clouds.

Mars is only about half the size of Earth, but it has about the same land area because there aren't any oceans. There is water on Mars, though. The Viking lander, the U.S. Mars probe, recorded water frost on rocks at its landing site. Scientists believe that the channels and meandering valleys on Mars may be evidence that there was once running water. And it's believed that there may be enough water trapped as ice to be collected, melted, and used by explorers while they're on the planet.

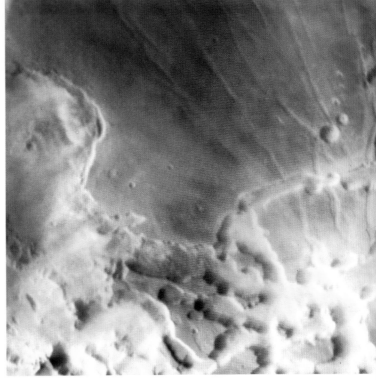

Mars has two moons, Phobos and Deimos, and Mars mission planners are considering including a visit to Phobos. Because they have odd, lumpy shapes and appear to be made of very dark-colored material, scientists believe these moons were asteroids captured by Mars's gravitational pull. Or according to one theory, they were one asteroid that broke in two. Either way, visiting Phobos would provide explorers a chance to take a close look at an asteroid.

Phobos is much closer to Mars than Deimos. It makes one revolution of the planet every seven hours and thirty-nine minutes. Deimos takes thirty hours and eighteen minutes to go around Mars. Scientists estimate that because Phobos is close enough to the planet to encounter its thin atmosphere, there is a small amount of drag on this moon. And it's likely that after another hundred million years or so, this drag will slow down Phobos enough that it will crash onto Mars's surface.

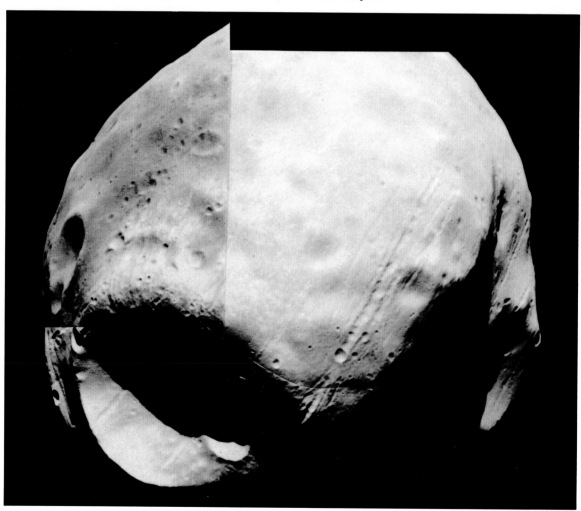

Now you know some of the ways in which people have already explored space and ways in which space pioneers are preparing to go farther, stay longer, and accomplish more. Eventually, people will move into space, living full-time aboard space stations and in colonies on the moon or other planets or even on asteroids. The technology necessary to make these pioneering efforts possible is being developed even as you read this book.

Earth need no longer be the limit of your dreams and goals. The space frontier is opening. You can help develop the equipment and tools that will make it possible to live in space and to work there. You may even want to go yourself.